The Unexplained

MONSTERS

By
J.M. Sertori

Please visit our web site at: www.garethstevens.com
For a free color catalog describing Gareth Stevens Publishing's list of high-quality books and multimedia programs, call 1-800-542-2595 or 1-800-387-3178 (Canada).
Gareth Stevens Publishing's Fax: (414) 332-3567.

Library of Congress Cataloging-in-Publication Data

Sertori, J.M.
Monsters / J.M. Sertori. — North American ed.
p. cm. — (The unexplained)
Includes bibliographical references and index.
ISBN 0-8368-6266-X (lib. bdg.)
1. Monsters—Juvenile literature. I. Title. II. Series.
GR825.S47 2006
001.944—dc22 2005044629

This North American edition first published in 2006 by
Gareth Stevens Publishing
A Member of the WRC Media Family of Companies
330 West Olive Street, Suite 100
Milwaukee, WI 53212 USA

Gareth Stevens editor: Monica Rausch
Gareth Stevens art direction: Tammy West

Picture Credits: t = top, b = bottom, c = center, l = left, r= right, OFC = outside front cover, OBC = outside back cover, IFC = inside front cover
Ann Ronan@Image Select; 4tl, 28bl, 29cr. AKG; 5tr, 4/5b, 6b, 6c, 8/9b, 8/9c, 9cr, 9tr, 10cl, 13bc, 12/13c, 14tl, 15r, 16tr, 17br, 18/19(main pic), 19cl, 19tl & 34, 23c, 24c, 24cr, 25, 26tl, 31c. CFCL; 22l. Corbis; 11tr, OBC & 12c, 15cl, 23tr. Et archive; 22/23tc, 28/29t. Fortean Picture Library; 4/5c, 13tr, 14/15c, 16/17c, 18tl, 20c, 20b, 26tl & OFC(inset pic), 26/27bc, 27c, 27, 31tr, 31bc, 33b. Images CWP; 12/13t, 17tr and OBC, 28tl. The Kobal collection; 8tl, 23bl, IFC, OBC, 24tl, 24b. Mary Evans; 26/27c. Planet Earth Pictures; 10tl, 10/11br, 19r, 28/29c, 33tc. Rex features; 21tl, 30/31c, 30, 30tr, 32bc. Science Photo Library; 32tl. Spectrum; 4bl. Telegraph Colour Library; OFC, 6/7r, 6tl, 10c, 10/11tc, 20tl, 20(main pic), 32cr, 32/33tc. Werner Foreman; 14b.

Printed in the United States of America

1 2 3 4 5 6 7 8 9 10 09 08 07 06

CONTENTS

What Is a Monster? 4-5

Natural Monsters 6-7

Classical Monsters 8-9

Dragons 10-11

Mixed Monsters, Family Beasts 12-13

Little Monsters 14-15

Giants 16-17

Vampires 18-19

Werewolves 20-21

Demons and Devils 22-23

Frankenstein and the Living Dead 24-25

Lake Monsters 26-27

Sea Monsters 28-29

Great Apes 30-31

Modern Monsters 32-33

Did You Know? 34

For Further Information 34

Glossary 35

Index 36

FANTASIES OF TERROR

Fear of the unknown has captured the human imagination for centuries. Since ancient times, we have imagined powerful images of terrifying creatures, from giants and werewolves to dragons and vampires. Discover the monsters that may—or may not—be products of the human mind.

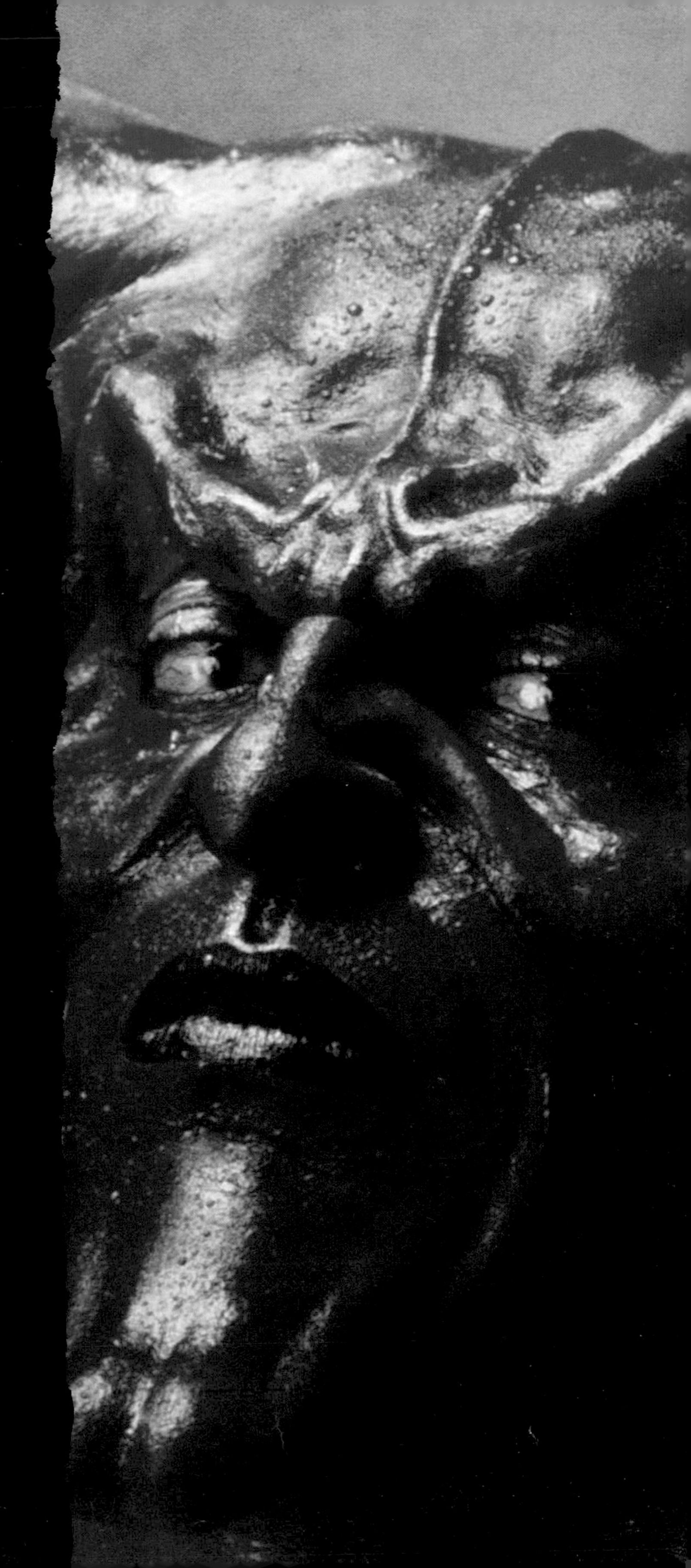

WHAT IS A MONSTER?

When people are faced with an unfamiliar object or animal, when they misunderstand causes for events, or even when they just cannot see in the dark, they can become afraid. In the past, our fears were often justified; before we knew more about our environment, Earth appeared to be an extremely unpredictable, and therefore scary, place. Events such as earthquakes and volcanic eruptions created more fear when they were unexplained. Wild animals could appear out of nowhere. Even today, we still have instinctive fears of the unknown or unexplained. For example, many people continue to be afraid of the dark because it represents the unknown. With the lights off, we cannot see what is around us, and our other senses can become confused. The human mind fills in gaps. We begin to hear and see things that do not exist—we create monsters.

FREAKY FORESTS

Forests can be homes to unknown creatures and can be easy to get lost in. For our ancestors, forests could hide enemy attackers or animal predators. Forests also could be places where, if one were hurt or injured, one could possibly never be found. People who wandered off a path into the "dangerous" forest did so at their own risk. The old tale of Little Red Riding Hood (above) helped warn children about these dangers. On the way to her grandmother's house, Red Riding Hood forgets her mother's warning to not stray from the path. She wanders through the forest and very nearly becomes a wolf's dinner.

TOOTH AND CLAW

This cat (right) is displaying its fangs because it is either scared or angry. The message it sends its viewer, however, is that it is a dangerous creature, ready to attack. Most people respond to danger signals, such as bared fangs, by becoming afraid and possibly running away. Fear is a natural protector, and the impulse to run has saved many lives.

IN THE MIND'S EYE

Generations of people have created and added to the many myths of dragons, werewolves, vampires, and devils. Over time, the numerous stories have helped these creatures become more real in the minds of humans. This creature (left) we now recognize as a dragon, but it has been created by human hands—and in the human imagination. Many of the monsters that scare us are actually human inventions.

NIGHTMARES

When we sleep, random thoughts and concerns we try not to think about when we are awake can sometimes get jumbled together and produce nightmares. The scary creatures of our dreams can be images of our fears. This painting (right), *The Nightmare* (1781) by Henry Fuseli (1741-1825), illustrates fears of the unknown that can come out in dreams.

CAVE PAINTINGS

One of the earliest ways humans recorded information, such as events or stories, was through painted pictures on the walls of caves (below). Like all art, the paintings reflected the hopes, dreams, and fears of the painters. By drawing or symbolizing a powerful beast on a wall, a painter may have hoped to control his or her fear of it. Even today, talking about or giving a visible form to what scares us sometimes helps to make it less scary.

What do YOU think ?

Monsters may not be real, but our fears are. Monsters often, in fact, represent our worst fears. Stories of humans facing monsters and defeating them may help us confront our fears. When we see that a monster is destructible, we are no longer afraid of it, and when we investigate why we are afraid, we often can get rid of our fear.

NATURAL MONSTERS

Not all "monsters" are figments of the human imagination. Dinosaurs were perhaps the most fearsome creatures ever to have lived. Fortunately, these prehistoric monsters never shared Earth with us; they died out some 65 million years ago, long before humans arrived. The natural world, however, still has plenty of other fierce creatures to inspire a sense of the monstrous. The ancestry of some animals, such as crocodiles, can be traced back to the Mesozoic Era when dinosaurs lived. If we encounter these creatures roaming free in their natural habitats, the potential dangers facing us would be very real.

KILLER FISH?

Many people have a monstrous fear of piranhas (above). An entire school of these sharp-toothed fish can strip the flesh from a creature in the water within seconds. In Brazil in 1981, more than three hundred people reportedly were eaten alive by piranhas when a boat capsized near Obidos. Many experts, however, say that stories of piranha attacks are exaggerated. The fish usually eat only weak or injured animals.

What do YOU think?

Do mammoths still exist—are any of these creatures still living in Siberia? Some people claim that some are still living and point to remains found in Siberia as evidence. Others, however, believe this "evidence" is probably the remains of long-dead mammoths only recently dug out of ancient ice. Mammoths might be frightening, but many people are just as scared of creatures that exist today. Some animals are so different from us that we see them as monstrous. Their sharp teeth, their incredible speed, their enormous strength, or their gigantic size can scare us, but animals are not "monsters." Most animals are interested only in hunting for food, and humans often are injured only after they have encroached on an animal's natural habitat. In fact, many animals fear humans more than humans fear them.

TYRANNOSAURUS REX

Tyrannosaurus Rex (right), perhaps the most well-known dinosaur, was a huge, meat-eating predator. This dinosaur could grow up to 47 feet (14 meters) long and 20 feet (6 m) high. It weighed almost 8 tons and boasted fangs 6 inches (15 centimeters) long. These awesome creatures terrorized East Asia and North America, but, luckily for us, the last one died millions of years before humans arrived.

MAMMOTH FEARS

Elephants may be large and seem scary enough, but just imagine if they had extra long tusks and were hairy—imagine if they were mammoths! The bodies of prehistoric mammoths (above) have been found in the ice of Siberia in Russia. Some people in remote parts of Russia have reported seeing living mammoths, but their stories of sightings are difficult to prove.

CROCODILE TEARS

Around two thousand people a year fall prey to saltwater crocodiles (left). Crocodiles have been hunting by river banks for eons. In fact, they have been around far longer than humans. They are not our natural enemies; they usually attack only if we have invaded their natural habitat.

THE KING CHEETAH

The king cheetah (left), a cheetah with a tigerlike stripe down its back, was thought for many years to be an imaginary creature. It reportedly carried off people along the border of Mozambique in Africa. Rumors of the existence of this animal, called *mngwa* by the locals, were finally proven true when Paul and Lena Bottriel photographed one in 1975. Scientists now know a "king" cheetah is just a normal African cheetah with a rare gene that changes the pattern of its coat.

THE LION'S SHARE

Lions (below) and tigers are familiar creatures to us today. We see them on television and at zoos. In the wild, however, before guns and traps were invented, these big cats were greatly feared. Wise humans left them alone, even though a lion or tiger would only attack a human being if it was provoked. Like many so-called "monsters," they are more likely to be afraid of us than we are of them.

CLASSICAL MONSTERS

CLASH OF THE TITANS

The film *Clash of the Titans* (1981) presents a very different version of the legendary sea monster that comes to steal Andromeda, the daughter of an arrogant queen. In the film, the sea monster, called Kraken (above), is a huge, amphibious creature similar to the city-stomping Godzilla. In the original legend, the sea monster was whalelike. Andromeda was sent as a sacrifice to appease Poseidon, the sea god her royal parent had angered.

Greek and Roman classical mythology features many scary monsters. Some monsters, which represented supposedly magical forces, were created out of people's awe of natural phenomena, such as tidal waves and earthquakes. Other creatures gave a monstrous form to human characteristics. The vicious power of gossip, for example, was personified in the mythical creature Rumour, a winged being with a thousand eyes and a thousand ears. Even some of the English words we use for being scared are rooted in a classical language—Latin. The Latin term *monstrum* means something that is shocking or scary and designed to keep us from straying from a path, just as stories of monsters are sometimes used to warn children of the real dangers of disobeying, or straying from a path. *Horror* comes from the Latin term *horrere*, which means "to bristle." When we are frightened, our hair stands up on end and we "bristle."

MEDUSA

The Gorgons were three terrifying mythical creatures that had snakes for hair. They also had wings, claws, and enormous teeth. Two of them, Stheno and Euryale, were immortal, or could never die, but the most famous Gorgon was the mortal Medusa (below). Once a beautiful girl, she was turned into a monster by the jealous Greek goddess Athena. Medusa was made so ugly that one look at her face would turn men into stone. The hero Perseus defeated her by looking only at her reflection. He then was able to cut off her head. Even after death, however, the sight of her ugliness continued to petrify anyone who looked upon her.

THE MIGHTY MINOTAUR

According to Greek mythology, Minos, the King of Crete, kept the minotaur, a man with the head of a bull (left), trapped in the center of a great maze. He then demanded that the Athenians send seven boys and seven girls into the maze to be sacrificed to the minotaur. If they did not, the King threatened to invade Athens. The monster finally was killed by the Greek hero Theseus, who had disguised himself as one of the sacrificial victims. Theseus was in love with Ariadne, the daughter of the King of Crete. She had given him a sword and a roll of string by which he could retrace his steps through the maze after slaying the beast.

HEADY HYDRA

According to classical legends, the hero Hercules was sent to defeat the hydra, a snakelike monster with nine heads (right). Each time one of the heads of this monster was struck off, two more would grow in its place. Hercules, however, defeated the monster when he managed to cut off eight heads, and then burn the necks so they could not reproduce more heads. He buried the ninth, immortal head under a rock.

SIRENS

According to legend, mythical sirens lured seafarers onto deadly rocks with their beautiful singing. The hero Odysseus (also called Ulysses), however, managed to hear them and still escape their grasp. He filled his crew's ears with wax and tied himself to the mast of his ship so he could not be tempted. The sirens eventually were destroyed by Orpheus, who sung a sweeter song. Defeated, they flung themselves into the water, where they were turned into rocks.

What do YOU think ?

The ancient world was filled with myths and legends. Stories were told for entertainment, but they often were rooted in real events and dangers. The people of Crete, for example, worshiped a bull-god and often feared invasion. Over time, these facts probably developed into the fictional tale of the minotaur. The story of the sirens probably grew out of sailors' natural fear of dangerous rocks and strong tides that could pull them in. Other stories, however, simply were created out of exaggerated fears. What is more fearful than a snake? A snake with nine heads!

DRAGONS

Dragonlike creatures exist in the legends of many cultures throughout the world. According to Chinese legends, the image of a dragon was created when a tribe with a snake in its coat of arms conquered other tribes that had other animals in their coats of arms. With each conquered tribe, a new animal feature was added to the original snake. The resulting beast had the antlers of a deer, the body of a snake, the wings of a bird, and so on. Eventually, the Chinese had invented a creature like no earthly beast. The dragon symbol became so powerful that it was later used to symbolize the Chinese emperor. In European mythology, dragons were evil, serpentlike creatures that heroes needed to defeat. Some Native Americans also had legends of a dragonlike creature. Known as the Thunder Lizard, the creature possibly was inspired by Native Americans' discovery of dinosaur bones.

SNAKE IN THE GRASS

The snake (above) is seen in some cultures as a symbol of evil. Its forked tongue also has been viewed as a sign of telling lies.

THE EVIL SERPENT

In European mythology, dragons were seen as dangerous enemies and were often the personification of evil or even the devil himself. The term *dragon* has its origin in the Greek term *drakon,* meaning "serpent." The dragon usually was shown to be a serpentlike creature, similar to the serpent in the Bible's Garden of Eden. Here, Saint George (left) defeats evil in the form of a dragon.

EARTHQUAKES

In the past, when people found dinosaur fossils, they did not know how to explain them. Some people assumed the bones were the remains of giant creatures that lived near the center of Earth. When one of these sleeping giants shivered, the whole Earth would quake, causing earthquakes (right).

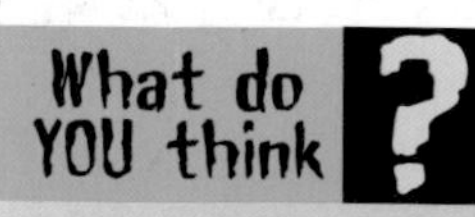

Until the causes of certain natural phenomena were understood, humans created monsters to explain terrible events such as tornadoes, waterspouts, and earthquakes.

A REAL DRAGON

In 1912, a 10-foot (3-m)-long lizard that ate pigs and goats, was discovered on several islands in the Indian Ocean. The new species of lizard (opposite) was the largest lizard in the world and was quickly named the Komodo dragon. In 1979, an expedition to New Guinea found archaeological evidence of an even larger lizard. Perhaps a live specimen of this species is still waiting to be discovered.

THUNDER AND LIGHTNING

In China, the word for *dragon* is also the term used to describe the sounds of thunder and the flash of lightning in the sky. To an ancient Chinese sage, lightning was caused by two dragons fighting in the sky. The snakelike image of a lightning flash (left) may help explain why Chinese dragons were depicted as long, snaking creatures. Storms were not the only natural phenomena attributed to the work of dragons; offshore tornadoes, called waterspouts, whisked water into great whirling spouts that were known as sea dragons. In the past, reports of bad weather often were misunderstood as the activities of supernatural creatures.

ASIAN DRAGONS

Unlike the dragons of European legends, East Asian dragons (above) are often good-natured. As long as they are respected, they can act with great kindness. According to some stories, a dragon is actually the spirit of a great person. If a person is great enough, he or she possibly can become an immortal spirit, or a spirit that never dies. Then, after many centuries, the spirit becomes a "dragonet" and dives beneath the earth to sleep. When it finally wakes, it is a "dragon," and it tears itself free to fly up to heaven.

SCARING YOUR ENEMIES

This suit of Japanese samurai armor (right) is designed to look monstrous. In the heat of battle, warriors needed all the help they could get. Horned helmets—or even spiked armor for their horses—helped terrify their enemies.

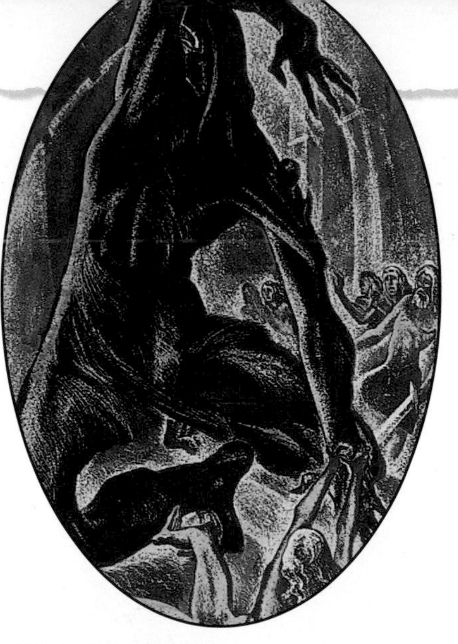

A KING'S DEFENSE

In the Old English epic tale *Beowulf* (about A.D. 1000), Grendel is a troll-like creature that plagues King Hrothgar's hall. Eventually, Beowulf, the tale's hero, slays him by tearing off his arm (above). In medieval England, warriors such as Beowulf were expected to defend their king's interests in exchange for weapons, food, and other goods. Their weapons often displayed the king's coat of arms.

HERALDIC BEASTS

Noble families often regarded their family symbols as guardian spirits. They also designed them as images (below) that would strike fear into their enemies.

MIXED MONSTERS, FAMILY BEASTS

In Europe in the Middle Ages, very few people could read and write. Noble families and public figures therefore used pictures in the form of coats of arms to symbolize and display their power. Images from coats of arms were made into seals to stamp and authenticate legal documents in place of written signatures. These images were also used on buildings, flags, and armor. A coat of arms often featured a powerful beast, such as a lion or bear. When families joined through marriage, their coats of arms were often united as well. The new united family's symbol would feature a new beast, with body parts taken from the beasts of the original families' coats of arms. The new "mixed" creature became a symbol of a larger, more powerful family.

GREAT GRIFFIN

The griffin (above) is part eagle and part lion. In heraldry—the study and design of coats of arms—the lion and eagle are both symbols of power and strength. Combined, they make a scary monster indeed. A remarkably similar creature—a tiger with wings that also symbolizes the super powerful—is found in Chinese culture.

CHIMERA

In Greek mythology, the chimera (above), a fire-breathing monster, had the hind parts of a dragon, the body of a goat, the forelegs of a lion, and the heads of all three. The origin of this fearsome creature can be traced to a volcano in ancient Lycia, a region on the coast of southwest Asia Minor. According to legends, this volcano had a fiery summit, lions in its upper forests, goats on its lower slopes, and serpents in the marshes at its foot.

What do YOU think ?

Was Grendel a real creature? Probably not, but as a symbol of an enemy tribe, he must have appeared to be a fearsome foe. Many monsters in heraldry are symbols of synergy, or the power gained through combining forces with others. The "mixed" monsters send a clear, threatening message to enemies; if an enemy crosses one family in a group, he crosses them all. Today, the image of a beast made of a mixture of species still inspires fear. Fictional tales of science experiments gone wrong, for example, often feature "mixed" monsters. In the science-fiction movie *The Fly* (1958) and the 1985 remake of the film, a laboratory accident causes a man and a fly to become one fearsome creature.

LITTLE MONSTERS

The mythologies of many cultures include stories of little people, such as gnomes, dwarves, elves, and leprechauns. Although little people may not seem "monstrous" in size, these small mischievous beings could still cause a great deal of harm. Sometimes they were seen as mean, misshapen old men who hoarded treasure. Other times, they were portrayed as demonic. Because of their small size, they could dwell in houses, in chinks in trees, or in other nooks and crannies. Some of the most famous little creatures are perhaps the Scandinavian Norse dwarves. They had their own king and were not unfriendly to humans, but they could be very vindictive. In fact, the Norse word *alfar* may have given us the English word *elf*.

FROM DJIN TO GENIE

Middle Eastern *djin*, or demons, were said to have been created out of fire two thousand years before Adam was made out of clay. They entered European mythology in the form of genies (above), trapped in small bottles. Their original destructive powers were lessened over time and eventually were confined to the granting of wishes.

DWARVES

Dwarves are found in the mythologies of many cultures. They were said to live underground or in rocks and to be guardians of Earth's precious metals and stones. Dwarves were sometimes believed to help human beings. Carved on this stone tomb (above), four dwarves are depicted supporting the sky over a dead Viking.

What do YOU think

How did stories of little people develop? Perhaps they can be traced back as far as the Iron Age. It is said that elves and fairies live in forests and are wounded by iron. These ideas may relate to how the ancient peoples of the Bronze Age culture were pushed into the forests and wilderness by invading Iron Age tribes. Other fairy tales may come from pagan religious beliefs that sometimes included beliefs in small, spiritual creatures. Another explanation may also be true: if a person wanted to explain away his or her own act of mischief, the person might blame it on an elf or dwarf. Of course, the mischief-maker would have to be small; if it was a giant, everyone else would have seen it. The sound of mice scurrying behind a wall may even have been used to support the tall tale!

FRIENDLY FAIRIES?

People often think of fairies as tiny, butterflylike creatures (right) described in many children's stories. In earlier times, however, fairies were creatures to be feared (below). Fairies were seen as creatures that lived in dark forests and were said to steal babies from their mothers' arms. They also would lure unsuspecting travelers to their doom. As symbols of temptation, they would convince a person to commit a sin without revealing that the person would later have to pay a horrible price.

ELVES

Although sometimes allies of humans, elves were known to be unreliable; they were likely to go back on bargains and twist the words of promises. In the Middle Ages, when a child was born lifeless or with a disability, people believed fairies or elves had swapped the human child for one of their own—a "changeling." Some stories say elves are hurt by iron, a metal said in China to "wound the eyes of dragons."

KOBOLDS

In German legends, a kobold (right) is a kind of dwarf said to live in mines. It was said the kobolds wanted to keep Earth's riches for themselves and would do everything they could to make life difficult for silver miners. They were blamed for cave-ins, explosions, and rockfalls, and miners lived in dread of their activities. The name for the silver-white metal cobalt may have come from these creatures' name.

What do YOU think?

Some people grow to be very tall, but that does not make them monsters. Tall people can suffer from a variety of health problems, including backaches and tunnel vision. Some people have suggested that Goliath may have had tunnel vision, and therefore he would not have been able to see a rock flying at him from the side. In mythology, some giants may have had no basis in reality but simply grew out of the need to explain strange natural phenomena. Fear of giants may also be left over from our childhood. While growing up, a child is loomed over by adults who are so much taller than they that, to a tiny child, they could seem like giants.

GOLIATH'S FALL

In the Bible, David, the future king of Israel, felled Goliath, a giant and a champion of the Philistines, with a single stone slung at Goliath's forehead . He then killed Goliath with Goliath's own sword (below right). Goliath was said to stand over 9 feet (2.7 m) tall.

REAL GIANTS?

In Kashmir, Professor James Ricalton (center) appears to have met two towering, "giant" men. But how *giant* are they? The men are certainly taller than average, but they may be made to look even taller in this photograph. For example, Ricalton has taken his hat off, but the two "giants" wear turbans, which add to their height. The giant to the left of Ricalton also appears to be standing slightly forward, making him closer to the photographer and therefore larger in the photo. The image is impressive, but parts of it are cosmetic.

GIANTS

Perhaps more frightening than the stories of small, devious people are the stories of gigantic people. Stories of giants may have some basis in reality, since some people do grow very tall. The world's tallest man on record is Robert Wadlow, who was 8 feet 11 inches (2.7 m) tall when he died in 1940. Wadlow, however, is tiny compared to the giants of mythology. In Greek legends, Atlas was large enough to carry the entire world on his back. Britain's mythical King Arthur slayed the giant of Mont St. Michel, who was said to kidnap women. Ancient Greeks also told stories of the gigantes, giants said to be imprisoned in volcanoes. The Greeks may have found it more reassuring to believe a volcanic eruption was the planned work of giants than to think the forces of nature were unpredictable. Large natural phenomena, such as the Giant's Causeway, said to be the ruins of a gigantic road built between Ireland and Scotland, are sometimes seen as proof of the existence of giants.

CYCLOPES

The cyclopes were one-eyed giants who, according to Greek mythology, enjoyed the taste of human flesh. They also were the supposed builders of the great prehistoric walls found in parts of Greece and Italy. Cyclopes often were featured in the tall tales of seamen. Both Odysseus, the mythical king of Ithaca in Greece, and Sinbad the Sailor from Arabian legends had encounters with cyclopes.

GIGANTIC THREATS

Some giants are designed to make people feel small and vulnerable. This huge foot is one piece of what was an enormous statue of the Roman emperor Constantine the Great (A.D. 306-337). It was specifically built to a massive size to remind people that Constantine was boss. Great size or the illusion of it is also used in the natural world to scare away potential predators. Puffer fish "puff" themselves up when threatened, so they appear to be bigger than they are.

VAMPIRES

Perhaps the most famous vampire is Count Dracula, the vampire from the novel *Dracula* (1897) by Bram Stoker (1847-1912). Legends of vampirism, however, existed long before that novel was written. According to some legends, a vampire is the spirit of a dead criminal or heretic—a person who holds different religious beliefs than those of an established church. In most stories, a vampire comes out of its grave at night in the form of a bat. The vampire then bites people's necks while they sleep and sucks their blood. The victims of the vampire often reportedly become vampires themselves. Some myths say vampires cannot be reflected in a mirror because they have no soul.

VLAD THE IMPALER

Vlad III (1431-1476) of Walachia may have provided some inspiration for Bram Stoker's *Dracula*. Born in 1431 in Transylvania, Vlad (below) was a brutal warlord reputed to have killed over a hundred thousand people. Stories tell of him nailing hats to people's heads, skinning them alive, and, most famously, impaling them on upright stakes—for which he earned the nickname Vlad the Impaler. He also was called *Dracula*, meaning "son of the dragon." His behavior made some people think he had sold his soul to the devil and led to rumors that he would never be admitted into heaven. He was murdered in 1476, but after his death, his tomb was reported empty, and the legends began.

ELIZABETH BÁTHORY

The character of Bram Stoker's Count Dracula may have been based on two historical figures: Vlad the Impaler and Countess Elizabeth Báthory (above). Countess Báthory was arrested in 1610 for murdering young girls. She reportedly believed bathing in the blood of her victims would keep her looking youthful.

A REAL BAT

The vampire bat (below) is a real species of bat. To feed, this bat scrapes a hole in an animal's skin and drinks its blood. In this way, the vampire bat is similar to a mosquito—only bigger. Its blood-drinking, however, became associated with vampirism and affected its name.

MODERN MYTHS

Modern vampire myths say vampires can change from a human form to wolves, bats, or even clouds of gas. In movies (opposite) and on television, vampires often have long fangs for sinking into human flesh and drinking blood, and they have to stay out of sunlight. They can be killed only by a stake through the heart.

What do YOU think ?

Stories of vampires may have their roots in several fears—and facts. The stories may be a way to illustrate the fear people have of a powerful person who can abuse others under his or her control. The stories also portray a fear of the dead and a fear of what happens to the human body after a person dies. After death, a person's skin shrinks back slightly, making teeth and nails look longer. The person also appears pale, as if his or her body has been drained of blood. Perhaps these events may account for the image of pale, blood-seeking vampires with long fangs and fingernails. A cloud of gas rising over the decaying body of a dead person in a graveyard may also inspire tales of vampires rising from graves at night. Another fear that inspires these stories is the fear that an animal, such as a bat, can be possessed by the spirit of a dead person.

WEREWOLVES

A true werewolf is half man and half wolf. In many legends, a werewolf is a man who changes to a wolflike creature only at certain times. Legends of these creatures date back to prehistoric times. We can see in cave paintings that shamans, or spiritual leaders, were thought to have the power of shape-shifting—changing from a human form into an animal. Similar stories were told of the Vikings, who often wore wolf skins to strike fear into their enemies. In modern myths, such as the one shown in the film *Teenwolf* (1985), stories of werewolves have emotional elements. In these stories, werewolves are often afraid of not being loved and are ashamed of their dark side, which cannot be tamed. Some werebeasts are sad figures, in search of beauties to "tame" and love them.

FULL MOON FEARS

A werewolf supposedly takes on its beastly shape when there is a full moon—and supernatural forces are believed to be at their strongest.

What do YOU think ?

The idea of changing into a wolf—or, in some cultures, into a tiger, bear, or lion—may have come from the fear that all humans have an inner "wild" beast. The stories may show how afraid we are of leaving—or simply forgetting—the safety of "civilization" and plunging back into the what we have worked so hard to "tame"—our own animal natures. These stories, however, may also be a way for people to explain animal attacks. The wild animal could be a human enemy disguised as a beast. Werebeasts could also take the blame for human crimes—especially crimes committed when the bright light of a full moon made it easier for criminals to do their work.

THE FRENCH WOLF

The beast of Gévaudan (left) was thought to be a werewolf. From 1764 to 1767, this beast reportedly terrorized the French countryside. It was said to be the size of a cow, and it supposedly claimed the lives of over sixty peasants by the time it was killed—shot in the chest by a silver bullet. Its stomach was said to contain the collarbone of a young woman. Its carcass reportedly was buried, but it has never been found.

ANCIENT WOLVES

Certain mental illnesses once caused people to think they were beasts. People with *lycanthropy* reportedly not only believed they were wolves but could actually turn into wolves. Different places also inspired tales of different werebeasts. In northern Europe, stories were told of men who turned into bears, and in Africa, of men who turned into hyenas (left). The Greek historian Herodotus (*about* 480-425 B.C.) claimed the Neuri people of Sarmatia in northeastern Europe were sorcerers: "For each Neurian changes himself once a year into the form of a wolf, and continues in that form for several days, after which he resumes his former shape."

BEAUTY AND THE BEAST

Tales of men who look or behave like animals are not limited to stories of werewolves. In the novel *The Strange Case of Dr. Jekyll and Mr. Hyde* (1886), the civilized Dr. Jekyll changes into the beastly Mr. Hyde, who commits murder. In the fairy tale *Beauty and the Beast* (below) the beast is changed into a man after finally winning the love of a beautiful woman.

HYPERTRICHOSIS

An extremely rare disease called hypertrichosis can cause excessive amounts of hair to grow all over the body, as in these men (above) of Mandalay. People with this disease were often mistreated by the public. Some people even called them dogmen or werewolves.

THE WOLF OF THE WILD

Humans have always had an uneasy relationship with wolves (right). They often were feared because they hunted in packs. Wolves, however, will not attack humans unless they are provoked. Today, many people see them as pests that kill valuable livestock.

KALI

Kali (above), the Hindu goddess of death, represents the unpredictability—and the inescapability—of death. According to some Hindu beliefs, if a person sacrifices an animal—or even another human—to Kali, the person will receive riches or other rewards. Kali usually is depicted as a red-eyed woman with four arms, wearing a necklace of skulls.

GURGLING GARGOYLES

Gargoyles (above) come in a variety of grotesque, often demonlike, shapes. Although they appear fierce, they actually are simple waterspouts used to drain water from roofs. In Europe in the Middle Ages, gargoyles were placed on roofs for several possible reasons. They may have been thought to scare off evil spirits.

DEMONS AND DEVILS

The Hindu word *deva* and the ancient Greek word *daemon* describe mythical creatures believed to have both good and bad natures. Over time, however, these words were adopted into the English language and changed into the words *devil* and *demon*—terms describing supernatural creatures that are believed to be completely evil. Some Christians also refer to the devil as *Satan*, which comes from the Hebrew word *shatana*, meaning "adversary." They consider Satan to be the supreme evil spirit—the enemy and tempter of humans and the ruler of Hell.

PAN

The ancient Greek god Pan (above) was half man and half goat. His image later became a model for many Christian images of the devil. The cloven hooves and the horns especially seem to have been carried over into modern devil images.

FALLEN ANGELS

According to some Christian beliefs, the devil once was a high-ranking angel who rebelled against God. He was thrown out of Heaven (right) and became Satan, the ruler of Hell. Other lesser angels who rebelled also were kicked out of Heaven and now serve Satan as demons. In the epic poem *Paradise Lost* (1667), John Milton (1608-1674) describes the angels' fall.

LUCIFER

"How art thou fallen from Heaven, O Lucifer." Some people believe this verse from the Bible's book of Isaiah originally referred to the arrival of the morning star, known in Latin as *lucifer*, or "light-bringer." The star arrived after the death of a Babylonian king. Over time, they believe the meaning of this phrase was changed to refer to Satan (right)—the fallen angel. Most people today associate the name *Lucifer* with evil.

What do YOU think?

Like fairies and sirens, demons and devils are symbols of temptation as well as symbols of evil. Devils and demons also were once associated with one's enemy. In the past, people at war often imagined themselves fighting evil when fighting their enemies. Tales of ancient wars fast became tales of demonic attacks.

FRANKENSTEIN AND THE LIVING DEAD

Many religions include a belief in some sort of life after death. According to some religions, after a person dies, the soul, or spirit, of the person continues to live but leaves the body. Myths about the "living dead" often involve the idea of a dead person's body coming back to life—either with or without a soul. These "living dead," called "zombies," are also said in some myths to feed on human flesh.

VOODOO ZOMBIES

According to some voodoo beliefs, certain voodoo sorcerers have the power to control zombies, or bodies of dead people that they have brought back to life. Some people believe, however, that these "zombies" were never dead; they are people who have been fed a certain medicine that make them appear as if they were dead.

CANNIBALISM

Some people of the South Pacific are said to have once practiced cannibalism. These people reportedly believed they could help their dead relatives continue to live in some way by eating their bodies after death. During the days of the European explorations of Africa and North America, explorers sometimes claimed the peoples they came in contact with were cannibals (left) and thus extremely "uncivilized"—even if no proof of cannibalism existed.

GALVANI'S EXPERIMENTS

In 1791, the Italian scientist Luigi Galvani discovered that by passing electricity through the legs of a dead frog, he could make the legs twitch (right). This experiment led to the idea that electricity could bring the dead back to life. Because electricity seemed so mysterious at that time, some people thought it was a divine force that gave life to dead things.

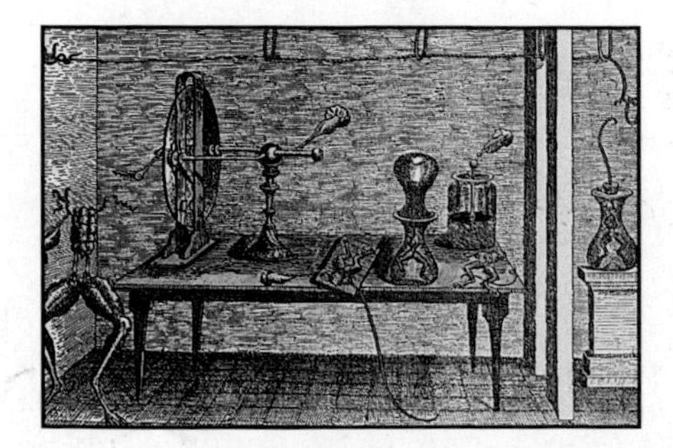

What do YOU think?

Many stories of the "living dead" are rooted in real but misunderstood scientific phenomena. For example, although electricity is not the divine life-giving force it was once thought to be, it does have a powerful effect on the human body. Doctors can send an electrical shock to the heart when it is beating out of rhythm, and the shock will set it back on track. The story of Frankenstein developed at a time when some doctors were beginning to study the bodies of the dead to learn more about why they died. People may have misunderstood these doctors' purposes. Mental illnesses, such as schizophrenia or catatonia, also were misunderstood. In the past, they were viewed as a possession by demons or by spirits of the dead.

DAWN OF THE DEAD

Some modern horror films (right) play on old zombie legends. In some films, such as *Dawn of the Dead* (1978), Hell is full, so the souls of the dead are forced to go back to the bodies they are supposed to have left behind. In other films, zombies seek out human brains to feast on, a strange craving perhaps inspired by cannibalism myths. Some people believed cannibals would eat the brains of enemies to gain the enemies' power.

FRANKENSTEIN'S MONSTER

In Mary Shelley's novel *Frankenstein* (1818), Dr. Frankenstein, a scientist, sewed together pieces of several dead bodies to create one whole body (left). He then shocked this body with electricity from lightning and brought his creation to life. The story of his creation has since inspired over fifteen films and several television programs.

LAKE MONSTERS

Scotland's famous Loch Ness monster appears to have many cousins around the world. Stories of lake monsters exist in Sweden, Iceland, Ireland, New Zealand, and Russia and in some African countries. In the United States, a sea monster called Champ is rumored to live in Lake Champlain, a lake that lies between New York State and Vermont. In Manitoba, Canada, the monster Manipogo is believed to inhabit Lake Winnipeg.

HEADS UP

Many photographs supposedly have been taken of the Loch Ness monster. This photograph (above), taken on Loch Ness in 1977, claimed to show the monster's head.

NESSIE

Ever since A.D. 565, when Saint Columba reportedly ordered a creature in Loch Ness to leave humans alone, the Loch Ness monster (right) has been one of the most famous beasts of Scottish folklore. "Nessie," as the monster is sometimes called, is said to have either a long neck on a large body or to be eel-like in shape. It often is claimed to be a prehistoric creature, dating back to the time of the dinosaurs.

HUMPS OR ROCKS?

This photograph (left) taken by Lachlan Stuart on Loch Ness in 1951 would seem to suggest that the Loch Ness monster has humps or is perhaps an eel-like creature snaking through the water— or could this just be a photograph of some rocks?

What do YOU think?

Many of the sightings of lake monsters have been discredited as hoaxes or proven to be other objects or animals—such as ducks, a dog swimming with a stick, or ripples on the lake caused by the wind. Scientists believe some prehistoric creatures may continue to exist in vast and deep ocean waters, but the chances are slim of any creatures surviving in the relatively small areas of lakes. Some people, however, continue to believe in their existence.

OGOPOGO

Tales of a creature living in Lake Okanagan in British Columbia, Canada, are perhaps rooted in the beliefs of local Native peoples. The Okanagan Indians believed a creature called *Na-ha-ha-itkh* lived in the lake, and they would offer it a meat sacrifice whenever they crossed the lake. Now known as Ogopogo, the creature is said to have a thick, snakelike body with humps. A replica (below) amuses tourists, some of whom hope to catch a glimpse of the creature. Ogopogo's story even inspired a song: *His mother was an earwig, his father was a whale, a little bit of head, and hardly any tail, and Ogopogo was his name.*

OMENICA DEL CORRIERE

6 Agosto 1962

La ragazza venuta da lontano

Il giallo di Hitchcock - a pagg. 6 e 7

ISSIE

Issie, a monster rumored to live in the depths of Lake Ikeda in Japan, is a humpbacked, dinosaurlike creature. A replica of Issie (above) welcomes Lake Ikeda tourists. Like Nessie, Issie has never been known to harm humans and seems to be very camera shy. Although many people have *almost* captured it on film, a proven photograph has yet to appear.

THE RIPPLE EFFECT

This ripple in the surface of Lake Ikeda could mean the lake monster Issie is about to surface—or could this just be a log?

MONSTERS OF THE DEEP

When William Shakespeare wrote *The Tempest* in the early 1600s, the British still were exploring the world outside of Europe. His play, which featured a supernatural storm, was perhaps inspired by tales of monsters (above) and shipwrecks told by sailors returning from the Americas. For the people of his time, monsters often were thought to be lurking in unexplored, unmapped areas. Any journey "off the map" was a journey into the unknown and into fear.

SEA MONSTERS

History is rich with stories of sea monsters. Sailors often returned to port with tales of fabulous creatures. Perhaps the most legendary beings were the mercreatures, said to have the body of a human and the tail of a fish. Sailors who supposedly spotted these creatures may actually have seen dolphins, narwhals, or dugongs—or perhaps just imaginary beings, created by minds tired from travel. Not everyone believes tales of sea creatures are fictional, however. Perhaps the creatures are rare animals that have existed since prehistoric times. The coelacanth, for example, is a fish species thought to have become extinct some 50 million years ago. In 1938, however, a living coelacanth was discovered along the African coast, and since then, scientists have found others in the very deep waters there. If these fish have survived for millions of years, some people believe other prehistoric creatures still may be cruising about in the unexplored depths of the oceans.

FANGTOOTH

This scary-looking fish (right), called a fangtooth, is actually small—only about 6 inches (15 cm) long. It also lives far from humans, in very deep ocean waters over 1 mile (1.6 km) deep. On the rare occasion when a dead fangtooth is washed up on shore, its teeth might scare humans into imagining what a giant version of this fish would look like.

What do YOU think

Whales and sharks may appear to be scary creatures, but they typically do not harm humans. They might, however, have inspired ancient tales of sea monsters. Today the oceans are still home to some "mysterious" creatures. Scientists, for example, still study the giant squid. A dead giant squid washed up on shore was 30 feet (9 m) long, but, based on sucker scars on sperm whales, scientists believe the squid can grow even larger. No one knows how large a full-grown giant squid might be.

OCTOPUSES

The octopus has always intrigued sea travelers. With eight arms, hundreds of suckers, and a powerful beak, it may appear to be one of the strangest creatures of the sea. Sailors have woven stories of giant octopuses large enough to swallow a human whole (left).

GIANT SQUID

This nineteenth-century Japanese print (right) shows a sea creature—probably a giant squid—as part of the legendary Dragon King's faithful army. Giant squid also may be the basis for tales of the kraken, a sea creature with long tentacles. Crews of whaling ships in the nineteenth century told stories of the kraken after sailors noticed that some whales they killed had scars from giant suckers. F. T. Bullen reported in 1901 that a harpooned sperm whale vomited up huge bits of a tentacle as thick as a man's body. Sperm whales are now known to feed on giant squid.

WHALES

A whale's enormous size often struck fear into the hearts of sailors. After all, early whalers (above) had only spears for hunting. These giant creatures, however, have no interest in harming humans. Whales were valued as a source of food and of raw materials for products such as candles and oil lamps. Some species were so valuable that they were hunted to the edge of extinction.

SHARKS

Some people consider sharks to be modern "sea monsters." Sharks, such as the blue shark (above), may look ferocious, but unless they are provoked, most sharks will leave humans alone. The whale shark is the largest known fish in the world, measuring 60 feet (18 m) long. This giant fish, however, does not eat people; it eats only tiny plant and animal organisms called plankton.

THE YETI

Some people living in the Himalayan Mountains of Nepal and India believe a giant ape-like creature (above), called the Yeti or the Abominable Snowman, lives in the mountain range. Parts of the steep, rugged mountains are so remote that people may find it easy to believe undiscovered creatures live there. The Yeti is supposedly a distant, ape-like relative of humans. In 1975, Janusz Tomaszczuk, a Polish hiker, claimed he was approached by an ape-like creature in the Himalayas. His screams, however, drove it away.

YETI'S FOOTPRINTS

Nobody has ever captured a Yeti, but a Yeti's footprints supposedly have been photographed. These large footprints (below) are deep and spaced far apart, suggesting that they were made by a tall, heavy creature. The creature that made them is certainly not human, but it could be the elusive Tibetan blue bear, a rare bear species that has never been seen by Westerners. This bear has been identified only through a few samples of bear skins, now in museums.

THE SCOTTISH SNOWMAN

This photograph was taken high up on Ben Nevis, the highest mountain in Scotland as well as in all the British Isles. Is it a Yeti living in Scotland? Or is it just a man in a gorilla suit?

GREAT APES

What might interest—or frighten—people most about apes is how how humanlike they appear to be. Stories of great, ferocious apes abound in history. In fact, tales of a real ape species—the mountain gorilla—once were regarded as pure fiction. In the twentieth century, stories of apemen such as the Yeti in the Himalayan Mountains, Bigfoot in the American West, and the Alma in Russia became more and more popular, and many people soon began to believe they were true.

BIG FEET

Photos like this one (above), taken in 1995, have been used by some people to prove that Bigfoot exists—and used by others as an example of a fake.

KING KONG

King Kong (1933), a classic horror film (right), tells the tale of a 50-foot (15-m) prehistoric great ape. The ape, named King Kong, is captured on a remote island and taken to New York City to be put on display. He escapes and terrorizes the city before finally falling from the Empire State Building to his death. Although he was ferocious, the filmmakers portray his death as somewhat tragic; if people had left him on his island home, he would not have caused so much destruction.

BIGFOOT

In 1967, Roger Patterson took this famous video (right) of Bigfoot, an ape-like being he claims to have seen in northern California. Its height is estimated at 6.5 feet (2 m). Some people suggest Bigfoot is actually *Pithecanthropus erectus*, a species believed to be closely related to humans and now extinct. They suggest it may still live in remote parts of the world.

What do YOU think ?

The wilderness may hide some yet-to-be-discovered species. The existence of a Scottish apeman on a small island is doubtful, but stretches of Canada and the Himalayas are large enough to hide undiscovered species. Both the Yeti and Bigfoot are reported to live in areas where no humans live. If they do exist, they would have little contact with humans, so they might be more afraid of us than we are of them.

MODERN MONSTERS

MINI-MONSTERS

Just as people in the past feared "little people," people today worry about the dangers that come in small sizes. We now know that under a microscope we can see scarier creatures than we could ever imagine—viruses, bacteria, and other tiny disease-causing or disease-carrying organisms. Even the ordinary head louse (above) can look fierce.

Although most people today are skeptical about the existence of monsters, people still have modern "monsters" to fear. Fear is an instinctive emotion that is meant to protect us. It makes us stay away from dangerous animals or dangerous situations. The monsters that scare us today are no longer dragons in the sea or goblins in the forests. The scientific, technological age has created its own monsters. We now can see the tiny monsters that make us ill. We can imagine the terror of machinery gone out of control, and we can picture the world after a nuclear attack. As long as dangers exist, we can imagine monsters that create them.

MONSTROUS FEARS

For some people, scary monsters exist in their everyday lives. These people have intense irrational fears called phobias. They cannot help feeling fear in certain situations or in the presence of certain animals. Claustrophobia, for example, is a fear of enclosed spaces. Acrophobia is a fear of heights; agoraphobia, a fear of open spaces; and arachnophobia, a fear of spiders. People with arachnophobia may *know* most spiders are harmless, yet they cannot help feeling fearful around spiders.

What do YOU think ?

Science has explained the causes of many of our past fears, but there always will be unknown phenomena that we have yet to explain. Every time we learn something new, we seem to also uncover another mystery—another possible monster and another scary story.

ALIENS

Earth may be mapped and millions of its creatures studied and recorded, but space is still in many ways a mysterious place. Some people believe the monsters of the future will come from space. They believe aliens (opposite) are out there somewhere—and if they have not already landed on Earth, then they are on their way. Invasion and abduction by aliens are popular themes in science fiction stories. Aliens may serve the human need for an outside enemy on whom we can focus our fears.

RISE OF THE ROBOTS

Today computers and robots (left) are used to perform more and more tasks. Computers fly planes and operate hospital equipment. Robots help build cars and even perform surgical operations. What if these computers or robots break down? Or, worse yet, what if these machines decide to run by themselves—without human control? Authors and filmmakers have played on these fears. Stories abound of machines taking over the world, controlling or even killing humans.

THE ATOM

The atom is one of the tiniest building blocks of the Universe; all matter is made up of atoms. The discovery that we could split the atom into even tinier parts led to the development of the most devastating weapons of all time—nuclear weapons (right). These weapons are perhaps the most terrifying monsters of the modern world.

DID YOU KNOW?

When Greek ruler Alexander the Great marched his army home from India, he instructed his men to scatter giant weapons and pieces of armor along the banks of the rivers they crossed. The giant weapons and armor were designed to scare any attackers who might cross the rivers after them.

According to Chinese folklore, a person can calm rough waters by throwing in an iron object to wound the dragon beneath the surface. The dragon supposedly causes the waves.

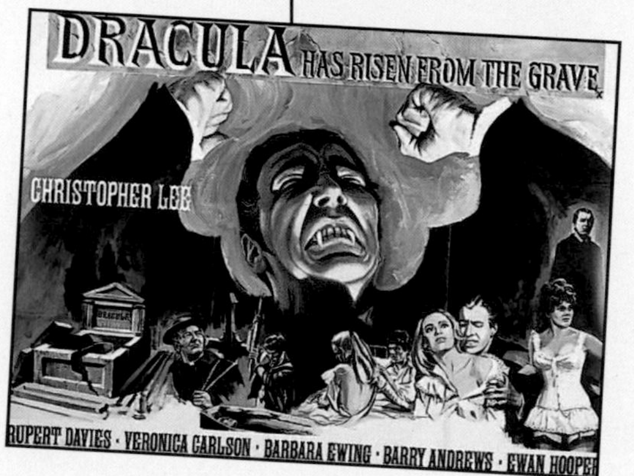

Apollyon (or Abaddon), the Angel of the Abyss, is a demon said to be so frightening that even sorcerers who summon him risk being literally "scared to death."

Maximinus I was 8 feet 6 inches (2.6 m) tall and had superhuman strength. His size and strength helped him rise in the ranks of the Roman army. When he was made emperor, however, in A.D. 235, this giant warrior was so brutal and cruel that his own men murdered him three years later.

According to popular myths, vampires can be defeated by sunlight, silver blades or bullets, holy water, or garlic. Some myths claim that to destroy a vampire, one must behead it with a gravedigger's spade and bury it at a crossroads.

The edges of the roofs of Chinese temples are curved upward, like ski jumps, so any demons falling from the sky would be flung away from the temples—and away from humans.

According to an old Danish story, a ferocious bear killed sixty horses and six men in Ofodens Praestegjeld before it was hunted down and slain. It was found to be wearing a man's belt, although nobody could explain why. Was it a werebeast?

In 1975, Sir Peter Scott, a prominent naturalist, gave the Loch Ness monster a Latin name, *Nessiteras rhombopteryx*, even though it has never been caught, examined, or properly photographed. The name later was found to be an anagram of "monster hoax by Sir Peter S."

FOR FURTHER INFORMATION

WEB SITES

National Geographic Kids: The Search for Monsters of Mystery **www.nationalgeographic.com/ngkids/9903/monsters/map.html**

NOVA Online: The Beast of Loch Ness **www.pbs.org/wgbh/nova/lochness/legend.html**

Vampires: Fact or Fiction **library.thinkquest.org/5482/**

Woodland Park Zoo: Komodo Dragons **www.zoo.org/komodo/komo_flash.html**

BOOKS

Gentle, Victor, and Janet Perry. *Monsters* series (Gareth Stevens)

Gorman, Jacqueline Laks. *X Science* series (Gareth Stevens)

Twist, Clint. *The Search for Life in Space*. Science Quest series (Gareth Stevens)

Weber, Valerie J. *Coelacanth: The Living Fossil*. Weird Wonders of the Deep series (Gareth Stevens)

GLOSSARY

adversary—person who opposes or attacks; enemy; opponent

amphibious—able to live on land and in water

ancestry—the humans or other animals in a family that came before

appease—satisfy; make peaceful or calm

authenticate—prove true or prove worthy of acceptance or belief

coat of arms — a design that is used to represent a family or group and is usually displayed on shields or military clothing

encroached—gradually moved beyond set limits and took over; invaded

environment—the surroundings of living things that affect how they grow and develop

extinction—the condition of having died out completely

gene—a tiny part of an animal or plant that determines what characteristics the animal or plant will have and what it will pass on to its offspring

habitat—the place where a plant or animal typically lives and grows

mortal—able to die

mythology—a set of stories, untrue or unproven, that usually develop over time and are passed on to explain a practice or belief

nuclear weapons—weapons whose explosive energy comes from the splitting or joining of the nuclei, or positively charged parts, of atoms

organism—any organized body of interdependent parts that work together to form a living being

origin—the source or the beginnings of

pagan—relating to a religion involving the belief in more than one god

personified—gave human characteristics or a human form to

phenomenon (*pl.* phenomena)—an act or an object perceived by the senses; a rare event

sacrifice—destroy or give up something valuable as an offering to satisfy a powerful person or being

sage—a wise person who is respected for his or her good judgment

skeptical—doubting; not believing

sorcerers—people thought to have magical or supernatural powers

species—a group of plants or animals that have similar characteristics

specimen—one of a group of plants or animals that is studied and treated as if it represents the group

supernatural—not being of the visible, earthly world; ghostly

unpredictable—not able to tell the result of in advance; having no set pattern and no fixed result

vindictive—wanting revenge or wanting to cause harm in return for an earlier injury

INDEX

Abaddon 34
Abominable Snowman 30
Alexander the Great 34
aliens 32
Alma 31
Andromeda 8
angels 23, 34
apes 30-31
Apollyon 34
Ariadne 9
Arthur, King 17
Athena 8
Atlas 17
atoms 32, 33

bacteria 30
Báthory, Elizabeth 19
bats 18, 19
bears 20, 30, 34
Beauty and the Beast 21
Beowulf 12
Bigfoot 31
Bullen, F. T. 29

cannibals 24, 25
cave paintings 5, 20
Champ 26
changelings 15
cheetahs 7
chimera 13
China 10, 11, 15, 34
Clash of the Titans 8
coelacanths 28
Columba, Saint 26
computers 33
Constantine the Great 17
crocodiles 6, 7
cyclopes 17

David, King of Israel 16
demons 14, 22-23, 34
devils 4, 10, 22-23
dinosaurs 6, 10, 26
djin 14
dolphins 28
Dracula, Count 18, 19
Dragon King 29
dragons 4, 10-11, 13, 15, 32, 34
dugongs 28
dwarves 14, 15

earthquakes 10
electricity 24, 25
elves 14, 15
Euryale 8

fairies 14, 15
fangtooth 28
fear 4, 5, 19, 29, 30
Fly, The 13
forests 4, 15
Frankenstein, Dr. 24-25
Fuseli, Henry 5

Galvani, Luigi 24
gargoyles 22
gas clouds 19
genetic experiments 13
genies 14
Gévaudan, beast of 20
Giant of Mont St. Michel 17
giant squid 28
giants 10, 16-17, 34
Giant's Causeway 17
gigantes 17
gnomes 14
Goliath 16
Gorgons 8
gorillas 30, 31
Grendel 12
griffin 13

hairy men 21
heraldic beasts 12, 13
Hercules 9
Herodotus 20
horror 8
Hrothgar, King 12
hydra 9

iron 14, 15, 34
Issie 27

Kali 22
Kashmir 16
king cheetahs 7
King Kong 31
kobolds 15
Komodo dragon 10, 11
kraken 8, 29

Lake Ikeda 27
leprechauns 14
lions 7, 13, 20
Little Red Riding Hood 4
living dead 24–25
Loch Ness monster 26, 34
Lucifer 23

mammoths 6
Manipogo 26
Maximinus I, Emperor 34
Medusa 8
mercreatures 28
Michael, Saint 10
Minos, King of Crete 9
minotaur 7
monstrum 8

narwhals 28
Neurians 20
nightmares 5
Norse mythology 14
nuclear weapons 33

octopuses 28
Odysseus 9, 17
Ofodens Paestegjeld 34
Ogopogo 26
Orpheus 9

Pan 23
Paradise Lost 23
Patterson, Roger 31
Perseus 8
phobias 32
piranha fish 6
Pithecanthropus erectus 31

Ricalton, Professor James 16
robots 33
Rumour 8

samurai warriors 12
Satan 23
Scott, Sir Peter 34
serpents 10
sharks 28, 29
Shelley, Mary 25
Sinbad the Sailor 17
sirens 9
snakes 9, 10

spiders 32
squid 28, 29
Stheno 8
The Strange Case of Dr. Jekyll and Mr. Hyde 21
synergy 13

The Tempest 28
Theseus 9
thunder and lightning 11
Thunder Lizards 10
Tibetan blue bears 30
tidal waves 8
tigers 7, 20
Tomaszczuk, Janusz 30
tornadoes 10, 11
Tyrannosaurus Rex 6

vampires 4, 18-19, 34
Vikings 14, 20
viruses 32
Vlad III of Walachia (the Impaler) 18, 19
volcanoes 13, 17
voodoo 24

Wadlow, Robert 17
waterspouts 10, 11, 23
werebeasts 20
werewolves 4, 20-21
whales 8, 28, 29
wolves 19

yeti 30, 31

zombies 24, 25